LINCOLNSHIRE DIALECTS

by

G. EDWARD CAMPION

With a Foreword

by

J. D. A. WIDDOWSON
The Centre for English Cultural Tradition and Language
University of Sheffield

RICHARD KAY
80 • Sleaford Road • Boston • Lincolnshire • PE21 8EU

CONTENTS

Acknowledgement

We are grateful to the Lincolnshire and Humberside Arts Association for permission to reproduce Noä Callers which first appeared in *Proof* – a magazine of new writing – summer 1975.
The cover design is by the author.

FOREWORD

Lincolnshire is remarkable for the strength and variety of its traditions, many of them founded on the old rural pattern of agricultural life which has declined rather more slowly there than in most other counties. The main railways and roads running north-south have bypassed much of Lincolnshire and it is only in the past half century or so that the older ways of life have changed so dramatically. The advent of the new Humber bridge with its promise of easier access, especially to the northern part of the county (now South Humberside) will also bring about a further erosion of the words and ways which have helped to give Lincolnshire people their sense of identity, of belonging. Changes in boundaries and local government mean corresponding shifts of attitude and a reorientation of local identification and allegiance. At such times the older patterns of life and behaviour are modified to adapt to the new circumstances, but old habits die hard and many of the traditional ways will remain, founded for example on features which do not change such as the division between the Wolds and the Fens. Indeed, some of these older patterns may well be strengthened by the threat of change which local people might well accept as a challenge and strive to preserve and capitalise on those traditions which they value. As outmoded forms are modified or swept away some of the older patterns remain as a firm basis on which to build new attitudes, modes and relationships essential to progress.

Nowhere is change more obvious than in local speech. Lincolnshire is justly famous for its rich variety of speech forms which have received considerable attention in the past, notably in the works of E. Sutton, R. E. G. Cole, Jabez Good, Edward and Mabel Peacock, Mrs. E. Gutch and, more recently, Mrs. E. H. Rudkin. Many of these have also studied the folklore of the county, while Lincolnshire folksongs have been extensively collected by such well-known scholars as Percy Grainger. What is surprising, and also disquieting, is that so little was written on the language of Lincolnshire in the first sixty years of this century. The Leeds *Survey of English Dialects* amply indicates the richness of the material which still exists and which has been the subject of such full and detailed studies as the M.A. dissertation, unfortunately still unpublished, of Stanley Ellis of the School of English at the University of Leeds, who undertook the bulk of the fieldwork for that Survey. Perhaps it was felt before that time, as so often happens in such studies, that all the work had been done. A glance at any of the older published sources, however, will immediately confirm that the earlier writers merely scratched the surface of the subject. Dialect, like all other forms of language, is constantly changing and evolving and its development needs to be monitored continuingly.

It is particularly heartening, in view of this, to note the upsurge of interest in Lincolnshire language and folklore during the past two decades and to witness the publication of Mr. Campion's book on the dialects of Lincolnshire. Ted Campion needs no introduction to Lincolnshire readers and indeed is also well known outside the county, especially for his work on Tennyson's dialect poetry. He is the author of *A Tennyson Dialect Glossary*, and regularly broadcasts about and gives public readings of Lincolnshire dialect poems as well as writing and publishing poetry himself. He has a passionate interest in Lincolnshire language and traditions and his obvious enthusiasm is infectious. I first met Ted Campion at an archaeological "dig" organised, like so many others in the county, by Mrs. Rudkin, who introduced us. Since that time he has regularly contributed material on local speech and lore to the Archives of the Centre for English Cultural Tradition and Language at the University of Sheffield, each contribution meticulously written, with appropriate illustrations, in his enviably elegant handwriting. These contributions, and the very handwriting itself, bear testimony to Mr. Campion's pride in his Lincolnshire upbringing, his pride in being a Lincolnshireman. Born at North Somercotes, he has, except for war service, lived and taught in the county all his life, observing with a keen eye and always aware not only of what people say but also of the way they say it. Perhaps the fact that he was brought up by his grandparents, two generations older, as it were, helped to arouse his interest in local speech. Whatever the reason, this interest has been fostered and extended and this book bears witness to its strength.

George Ewart Evans has said that the man who has lived through and experienced and paid close attention to certain aspects of life which have been central to his interests, such as a traditional craft or trade, is the man best qualified to tell us about those experiences. Ted Campion was not only born and raised in the language and traditions of Lincolnshire but has made them a central interest throughout his life, Much of what he writes here is gleaned from his own careful observation of life and work in his home county. It is my hope that those who read this book will be reminded of their heritage and consider its functions in our changing world. Better still, I hope others will be encouraged to follow Ted Campion's example and document those aspects of Lincolnshire language and life which they know themselves.

J. D. A. WIDDOWSON.

The Centre for English Cultural
Tradition and Language,
the University of Sheffield.

July 1976

To my wife

INTRODUCTION

The 1974 reorganisation of our country for the purposes of Local Government has brought about many changes. New counties like Cleveland and Avon have been created, some have been mutilated, and Rutland and Huntingdon have disappeared. Lincolnshire has lost a large area in the north which has now become South Humberside, and this includes the Isle of Axholme on the west bank of the Trent. The rearrangement upset long-standing boundaries that had enclosed communities with common cultures and interests, often jealously guarded.

Lincolnshire was basically an agricultural county and the local dialects had much in common as they dealt with the practical business of day-to-day rural living and did not venture very far into the realms of abstract ideas. By the time the boundaries were being re-drawn the County was becoming industrialised and the words my grandfather used on the farm were no longer adequate. Under the combined influences of almost a century of free education, the introduction of radio that brought a standard form of English into homes where a regional dialect was spoken, the invention of the internal combustion engine with improved communications, and two major wars that took men from their peaceful pursuits and replaced their parochial outlook with a wider vision, the dialects faded rapidly. For the purposes of dialect study we should ignore the new boundaries and regard Lincolnshire as the old county extending to the south bank of the Humber and across the Trent to include the Isle of Axholme.

The former Lincolnshire was the second largest county in England, so large that there were marked dialectal differences in the various regions. Indeed, it could scarcely be otherwise when we consider that Stamford in the south is only five miles nearer to New Holland in the north than it is to the centre of London, and we would expect the local patois to vary broadly as much if we travel the same distance in either direction. Dialectal variations are seen in numerous words, as for example those used to describe a sheep that has fallen on to her back and, because of her heavy fleece, is unable to get up. This is a serious situation as the animal would soon die if she were not helped on to her feet. In the Marshes she is said to be **farweltered,** in the north of the county it becomes **farwelted,** but in South Lincolnshire she is **cast.** In Mid-Lincolnshire a ladder is a **lether,** but in the Brigg area it is a **stee,** a survival of the Old Norse **stige.** This word is used through West Yorkshire right into Lancashire. Harrison Ainsworth uses it in his *Lancashire Witches*, but his spelling is **steigh.** The old-fashioned horse-drawn farm cart was constructed so that it could be tipped to discharge or **skell** a load by withdrawing a pin that secured the body to the shafts. Rather like a length of broomstick with a headless nail at each end, this pin was called a **juggle-pin** in the Louth area, a **type-stick** in the Fens south of Boston, but around Brigg it was a **thole-pin.**

Tennyson wrote his *Northern Farmer, Old Style*, the first of his Lincolnshire dialect poems, twenty-four years after the family left Somersby. It was published in 1861. He is recorded by W. F. Rawnsley in Canon H. Drummond Rawnsley's *Memories of the Tennysons* as saying,

> 'When I first wrote The Northern Farmer I sent it to a solicitor of ours in Lincolnshire.* I was afraid that I had forgotten the tongue and he altered all my Mid-Lincolnshire into North Lincolnshire and I had to put it all back.'

The transposition was not complete. The poem still contains the north county **hond, lond** and **understond** for 'hand,' 'land' and 'understand'. Tennyson read 'land' in 1881 to A. J. Ellis when he noted the reading phonetically for Ellis's book *On Early English Pronunciation* (*Part V.*).

The north Lincolnshire form was more frequently met with in the south Midland dialects and is to be found in Chaucer's Prologue to the Canterbury Tales:–

> 'And palmers for to seeken straunge strondes
> To fern halwes, kouthe in sondry londes.'
> (And pilgrims for to seek strange strands
> Of far-off saints, hallowed in sundry lands.)

Obviously there are wide variations in the dialects of the county, and to speak of THE Lincolnshire dialect is to over-simplify the facts. There is no such thing.

These notes have been written for the general reader, and they are intended to be neither pedantic nor unduly academic. The scholar is capable of more precise interpretation to suit his own requirements.

Pronunciation could have been indicated by the use of phonetic symbols, but the dialect sounds are somewhat complicated and expressed in this way would have been understood only by the phonetician, so a simpler method has been employed. The common Lincolnshire diphthongs are indicated by **ä,** which is a short a sounded separately from the preceding vowel but almost running the two together, so that **aä** is pronounced **ay-ä** in **raäke, eä** is **ee-ä** in **meät** and **oä** is **oo-a** in **roäd.**

Where the fourteenth century writers are quoted the spelling has been revised to the extent that the now obsolete letters **yogh**

---

* Possibly a Hattersley of Caistor who handled much of the Tennyson family business.

(sometimes pronounced as **g**, but at others as **y**) and **thorn** (with a **th** sound) have been given their modern equivalents in the interests of simplicity.

Old English, or Anglo-Saxon, refers to the language from the year 700 A.D. to 1150, Middle English 1150 to 1500 and Modern English from 1500 to the present time. These dates are arbitrary. Changes in language are gradual and not all scholars agree as to when the Middle English period began and ended, some thinking it started a little earlier and others extending it to well into the sixteenth century.

Some words used in the Lincolnshire dialects are not necessarily exclusive to the county, but they may be found in other parts of Britain that have been subjected to similar invasions and conquests, or that offer the same occupational opportunities because of comparative geographical conditions such as fertile plains or estuaries conducive to trade. As far away as Scotland the local speech contains certain words that the Lincolnshire dialect speaker employed in his vocabulary. In *Poetry of Northeast Scotland*, edited by James Alison (Heinemann Educational Books, published in 1976) we find words common to Scotland and Lincolnshire that include **loup,** 'leap'; **teem,** 'empty'; **happed,** 'wrapped'; **anew,** 'enough'; **dwined,** 'faded'; **sea-maw,** 'sea-gull'; **soss (about),** 'mess about'; **wudness,** 'madness'; and **lowsin' time,** 'time to stop work'.

I am very grateful to John Widdowson for his encouragement and advice, and also to Stanley Ellis who has given me invaluable guidance, particularly regarding Middle English references. I am most indebted to Edward Glover Campion (1847 - 1925) and Martha Ann Campion (1852 - 1936) who reared me in the dialect of the Lincolnshire Marshes and gave me a life-long interest in a very absorbing subject.

I

DIALECT AND STANDARD ENGLISH

It is difficult to define dialect to everyone's satisfaction as the subject is emotive. To the person who was brought up in a regional dialect-speaking environment it is understood, and the disappearing nuances, lost words and vowel sounds are remembered with nostalgic pleasure. The pedant tends to see dialect as uncouth, debased English that scorns the rules of grammar, hardly worth consideration and best forgotten. These extreme views are not easily reconciled. In an attempt to be as objective as possible, a convenient working definition could be :–

> Dialect is the speech of a group of people who share a common regional, occupational, or social oral communication that is different from that of other similar groups, but not so widely separated from them as to constitute another language.

We must, however, be aware that the geographical and occupational elements are closely linked. The rich land in Lincolnshire, so much of it flat and easy to cultivate, naturally produced a farming community with its peculiar occupational speech, while the discovery of ironstone at Frodingham attracted an influx of workers from many parts of the country, every group speaking its own dialect but uniting with others in a speech employing the terminology of their common occupation. These occupational dialects are spoken and understood by the trades and professions concerned, but are somewhat obscure to the outside, *e.g.* the bricklayer's **monkey** for hod, or the mower's **hugger,** a container to carry his rubstone on his belt. Occasionally words and phrases are accepted into standard English, but the transition can completely obscure their original meanings. 'The bitter end' is frequently used in everyday speech, but which end, and why is it bitter? In the old wooden ships stout posts called 'bitts' rested on the keel and supported the deck. The forward bitt was a convenient place to secure the end of the anchor chain, and that was known as the 'bitter end,' so to see a thing through to the bitter end simply means to the fullest extent. 'By and large' is another nautical expression describing a particular setting of the sails under certain wind conditions, but it is used by people with no knowledge of seamanship to mean 'more or less'.

Dialect is usually a spoken language of the manual workers as opposed to the classical language of the scholars. So much importance is placed on the written word as a means of communication that we tend to forget that language is basically spoken and writing is necessary only to convey thoughts to those who are absent, to future generations, or to make notes to remind ourselves about something we might otherwise forget. For thousands of years man communicated orally before the first scribe scratched his thoughts on a stone. Wonderful as some literature may be, the art of writing, particularly for the masses, is comparatively new. We must also remember that literature has become so advanced that it can be an art form divorced from spoken language. Who ever spoke like James Joyce wrote? Some modern poetry if taken at face value is unintelligible. My grandfather was illiterate but he led a happy and useful life, completely unconcerned about his inability to read or write as almost all his fellow-workers were similarly deprived. Literature for the Lincolnshire labourer hardly existed at the beginning of the present century, the only book being displayed in most homes being the family Bible, and that was rarely read. Covered with a lace-edged cloth, it was frequently used as a stand for an aspidistra. Methodists might extend their libraries to include *Josephus*, *Cruden's Concordance*, and some devotional reading, but these folk were usually the ardent local preachers. Since literature played so small a part in everyday life the dialect-speaking labourers kept their speech free from the influences of literary borrowings. The exception to this was the adoption of a few Biblical phrases and references learnt by heart in places of worship.

The Lincolnshire labourer was in dialect-speaking days often content to work for the whole of his life on one farm. Often two or three generations of one family would be employed by the same generations of farmers, though those who wished to move could always secure new **plaäces** at the local spring hiring fairs. These were held at the nearest market town which had a catchment area for labour of about ten to fifteen miles radius, so the migrations of the labourers, even if they were fairly frequent, were somewhat restricted and the dialectal differences they encountered were slight, so the local patois remained reasonably constant.

Modern standard English, on the other hand, contains a number of comparatively recent acquisitions from other tongues. We have been a nation of missionaries, traders, and conquerors extending our activities to all parts of the world. Our contacts with other languages and cultures resulted in borrowings from every continent. **Khaki** and **bungalow** come from India, **pyjama** from Persia, **garage** and **camouflage** came from France in the First World War, and **tobacco** from the North American Indian. **Tea** is from the Chinese Amoy dialect **t'e** and **coffee** from the Arabic **qahweh.** It is interesting to note that while some borrowings are accepted into our language others have very short lives. **Dekko** (look) came in from India early in the present century. It became popular in the 1914-18 War and then gradually declined. Though found in *The Concise Oxford Dictionary* it is rarely heard today. The Arabic **shufti** (look) was in use among the Forces in the Second World War, as was **mahlish** (I couldn't care less), but these were short-lived and were never really accepted into standard English.

English, like all living languages, is subject to fashions and fancies that ebb and flow like the tide. My grandmother always said 'adver**tise**ment,' but I was taught at school that the correct pronunciation was 'ad**ver**tisement' and so it has remained for the greater part of my life. However, many educated speakers on the radio and television are now using the old 'adver**tise**ment." '**Con**troversy' is now tending to revert to the once-favoured 'con**trov**ersy,' 'dis**trib**uted' is becoming '**dis**tributed,' 'con**trib**uting' '**con**tributing' and '**har**assment' is frequently pronounced 'har**ass**ment' Changing fashion not only dictates on which syllable a stress should be placed, but it determines to a lesser degree how words should be spelt. I was taught as a child that 'show' was the noun and 'shew' the verb, and I followed this rule for years, dropping the latter in favour of the 'show' verb when I realised that what I had been doing was now considered to be archaic. Those of my generation who were brought up on *Nesfield's English Grammar* never used the word 'rhyme' in reference to poetry. Nesfield insisted that the correct spelling was 'rime' and that 'rhyme' was nothing more than a confusion with 'rhythm.' Today it is accepted and 'rime' in this sense appears unfamiliar.

Being less influenced by fashion and more by traditional usage, dialect inclines to retain its form more than standard English does. The later is more likely to contain slang expressions and catch-phrases that are comparatively short-lived, soon to be supplanted by the next new fashion. Dialect has much deeper roots, most of its words having a very long ancestry.

The 'best' or most acceptable speech in this country is designated Received Pronunciation (R P), based on the speech of the educated people of the capital city. Up to the fourteenth century (when communications were poor) travel was an arduous enterprise not lightly undertaken. The Black Death resulted in a shortage of manpower so that it became easy for the labourers to break manorial ties and seek work in any place they fancied. The resulting population flow, together with improving communications and developing trade, made dialectal differences such an encumbrance that it became necessary to adopt one dialect as a recognised standard English, and the speech of the educated Londoner was accepted as the pattern. It is well to remember that basically Received Pronunciation is only an accepted dialect, and it could just as well have been derived from any of the other local forms of speech. The sounds of southern vowels and diphthongs are fewer and vary less than those from further north. Daniel Jones, in his English Pronouncing Dictionary, based on Received Pronunciation, gives exactly the same phonetic symbols for 'see' and 'sea', though in northern speech they are distinctly different, the **ea** in 'sea' being sounded nearer to the one in 'real'. He also uses the same diphthong in both words of 'go slow,' but further north these would rhyme with 'no know,' the opening of the jaws being slightly wider in pronouncing 'know' than it is for 'no'. A study of his dictionary produces numerous such examples. It is interesting to conjecture what Queen's English would have been like today if by some quirk of history York had become the capital of England and as such had dictated the nature of Received Pronunciation. We would without doubt have employed a much wider range of vowel sounds, diphthongs, and near triphthongs that would have enhanced standard English with more delicate nuances.

It is often erroneously assumed that the dialect speaker is just too lazy or too uneducated to speak 'good' English. Dialect is not slovenly English any more than slovenly English is dialect. The mother who asks her child, "Wan sum tweet?" (Do you want something to eat?) is speaking slovenly English, but it is certainly not dialect. Pronunciations and usages that are supposed to be bad and due to a lack of schooling are frequently regional speech backed by long traditions, and may be more correct than the modern English that replaces and condemns them. The Lincolnshire labourer invariably said, "You was." The grammarian maintains that 'you' is plural and therefore we should say, "You were", but if we are speaking to one person only with no one else in sight, from a practical point of view it is nonsense to say that 'you' is plural, and at one time its singular use was not unacceptable. Why can it not be both singular and plural like 'sheep', 'cannon', and 'deer'? (Though recently 'cannons' and 'reindeers' have come into use, but they would have been considered bad English in my youth.) The establishment of "You were" to be used at all times was a matter of fashion and etiquette rather than one of grammar. It was a French courtesy that we adopted into Middle English, giving plurality to one's superiors to indicate that they were more important than an ordinary man. The custom also survives in the Royal "We". Equals and inferiors were addressed as 'thou' or 'thee', but 'you' was reserved for one's 'betters'. This class distinction was illustrated by a Yorkshireman who retaliated to a person whom he considered was being too familiar, "Oo's thoo ti **thoo** me? I's **you** ti thoo."

The dialect use of 'went' for 'gone' was until recently heard in the south of Lincolnshire around Sutton Bridge, where the old people might say, "You never ought to have went." This sounds strange today, but it is an authentic survival. In *The Dancers of Colbeck* (c. 1375) by Robert Mannyng of Brunne we read:-

> 'They oute of that stede were went.'
> (They out of that place were gone.)

and Chaucer in his *Tale of Melibeus* writes:-

> 'Upon a day byfel, that for his desport he is went
> into the feldes to play.'

Richard Rolle of Hampole in *Love is Life* (1349) gives:-

'Wha fra me away war went.'
(Who from me away was gone.)

The word **war** is interesting here. It is an old form of 'was' that has survived in the dialect, but today it is rarely recognised as such. The person who says, "I war asleep," or "He war late," is sometimes accused of using 'were' incorrectly and with a slovenly pronunciation, but he is simply adhering to a previously recognised form of 'was'. Where Lincolnshire approaches Cambridgeshire it was common to hear **haves** for 'has'. e.g. "He haves two sons." This is a once correct usage that has lingered in dialect (I have, he haves), but standard English has adopted the contracted 'has'. In an anonymous poem, *Now Springs the Spray*, written about the year 1300 we read:-

'Mi lemman me haues bihot of louue trewe.'
(My beloved me haves vowed of love true.)

Compare this with *St. Matthew V.* 13 (*Authorised version*)

'If the salt have lost his savour, wherewith shall it be salted?'

Living language is in a state of flux, always changing, never static. Dialects are generally more stable in form than is English because they use traditional words and adopt few new ones. As 'the old order changeth' tools and methods disappear, taking the words that referred to them as they go. Some dialect words lose their significance and fade away, but English accumulates as it expands to accommodate a technological age governed by complicated political situations. Prior to the eighteenth century Latin was considered by scholars to be the classical language with a grammar so perfect that it should serve as an example for the construction of others. William Loughton in his *Practical Grammar of the English Tongue* (1734), had some doubts about this and condemned those who 'have attempted to force our language (contrary to its nature) to the method and rules of the Latin grammar', but the scholars who compiled English grammars were steeped in the Latin tradition and took little account of previous English usages. Thus the gap was widened between the now accepted Latinised English and the traditional tongue that survives to some degree in the dialects. Past grammarians have grafted on to the English language Latin based ideas such as the condemnation of ending a sentence with a preposition, though this was an English idiom well established by long tradition. This forcing of English into a Latin straight-jacket (at least as far as teaching is concerned) may have satisfied the pedants, but Julian Huxley wrote to *The Times* in 1890,

'My impression has been that the genius of the English language is widely different from that of Latin; and that the worst and the most debased kinds of English style are those which ape Latinity. I know of no purer English prose than that of John Bunyan and

Daniel Defoe; I doubt if the music of Keat's verse has ever been surpassed; it has not been my fortune to hear any orator who approached the powerful simplicity, the limpid sincerity of the speech of John Bright. Yet Latin literature and these masters of English had little to do with one another.'

Dialect differs from standard English in the formation of the past tenses of some verbs. In English the past tense of 'feed' is 'fed'. and that of 'read' is 'read' (pronounced 'red'), but 'weed' gives us 'weeded' and 'clean'. 'cleaned'. Lincolnshire people follow the former rule more closely and say, "I **wed** the garden this morning," and "Mary **clen** up after the party," giving a strong past tense. 'Know' becomes 'knew' in English, but the past tense of 'snow' is 'snowed', 'thaw' is 'thawed' and 'saw' (to cut wood) is 'sawed', though the Lincolnshire man would use **snew**, **thew** and **sew** (to rhyme with 'new'). The dialect tends to favour the strong forms of verbs that have become weak in standard English.

Rules have to be formulated if a language is to have a workable structure, so a grammar is essential, but it should be a servant and not a master. There is a danger that a traditional Latin based grammar may fossilise language at the expense of local valid variations if it is enforced by pedants who maintain so rigid a line that all development is stifled and all deviation suppressed.

II

THE VALIDITY OF DIALECT

Lincolnshire may be divided roughly into four main dialectal regions:-

1. That of the north, around Brigg.
2. The Mid-Lincolnshire dialect of the Louth, Horncastle, and Spilsby districts, extending towards Lincoln.
3. The southern speech of Boston and the Fens with some variations further south as we approach the Norfolk border.
4. An entirely different one in the Isle of Axholme where the Trent was such a barrier that the local speech was more related to that of the West Riding of Yorkshire than to the dialects of the rest of Lincolnshire.

These divisions must be somewhat arbitrary as no hard lines can be drawn between dialectal regions. They fuse together at the edges, giving an infinite number of variations, the appreciation of which depends upon the skill of the listener in recognising the delicate differences that occur.

Mid-Lincolnshire dialect contains more pure Old English than most. There are four main reasons for this. First we may consider the geographical and geological influences. Lincolnshire as a county was particularly isolated with the Humber on the north and the sea on the east. The River Trent on the west was an effective dialectal boundary that is crossed, even today, three quarters of the way through the twentieth century, by no more than three bridges at Keadby, Gainsborough, and Dunholme for half the length of the county. In the south we had the Fens that, before drainage, provided few good roads, most of the communications being poor and devious, known to the inhabitants but avoided if possible by travellers. So the only easy access into Lincolnshire was by the south-west corner through the Sleaford, Grantham, and Stamford areas. This resulted in the county being left to retain its speech, lore, and customs in some degree of isolation and with a great sense of independence. The men of Lincolnshire resented change and outside interference, whatever its source. The Pilgrimage of Grace started in Lincolnshire, and Henry VIII referred to the Pilgrims as 'the rude commons of one shire, and that the most brute and bestial in the whole realm'. The isolation of the county allowed the regional patois to remain reasonably untarnished by contact with outside influences.

Secondly, Lincolnshire was an agricultural society, the main power on farms being supplied by horses until after the First World War, and many of the farming methods changing little over the centuries. Consequently, many of the Old English words used on farms were adequate in my grandfather's day, until agriculture became more technical and people began talking about artificial insemination, brucellosis, and monogerm seeds. Words that were in use when I was a boy may be traced back to Chaucer and even to Old English. In North Somercotes an old drain was locally called the Eä, a pure Old English word that is erroneously given by cartographers on their maps as 'Eau'. We were taught that the **Eä** pronunciation was vulgar, but it was a dialectal survival standing securely in its own right, and more accurate than the French 'Eau' when applied to a north Lincolnshire drain. The Lincolnshire word **breed** for 'breadth', dialectally meaning a width of land worked, is found in Chaucer's *Knightes Tale*:-

> 'Al peynted was the wal in length and breede.'
> (All painted was the wall in length and breadth.)

Tennyson, in his dialect poem *Owd Roä*, uses the Old English word **wud** for 'mad':-

> 'An' screeäd like a Howl gone wud.'
> (And screamed like an owl gone mad.)

In *Sir Orfeo* (c.1350) we read:-

> ' . . . . and some lay wud ybounde'
> (. . . . and some lay bound because they were mad.)

The third reason why Lincolnshire speech has tended to retain its older forms is that the county has no universities and few other important centres of learning, so there has been no significant Latin infiltration into the dialects. The only instance I know is the colloquial **num-cumpus** for **non compos mentis**. In *The Northern Cobbler* Tennyson writes:-

> 'Sa like a greät num-cumpus I blubber'd awaäy o' the bed.'

Generally speaking, education was not appreciated in Lincolnshire as boys were expected to follow their fathers and work on the land. When I decided to do something different some of my contemporaries considered that I was stepping out of line and did not know my place. My grandfather's workmates told him, "Yah'll edicaäte that boy till 'e weän't work!" The attitude was that nothing mattered except hard, manual work, as illustrated in the jingle that was current at the beginning of this century:-

A HUNDRED YEARS OF FARMING.

1800.

Farmer's at the plough.
Wife's milking cow,
    Daughter's spinning yarn,
    Son's threshing in the barn,
All happy to a charm!

1900.

Father's gone to see the show,
Daughter's at the pian-o,
    Madam's dressed in silks and satin,
    Boy's at school a-larning Latin,
With a mortgage on the farm!

The fourth element in keeping the character of the dialects stable is that almost all the industry was near the western border of the county at Gainsborough, Lincoln, and Grantham, so there were few industrial terms to overspill into everyday speech. The Scunthorpe steel industry has grown up mainly within living memory when dialect terms were declining, so for our purposes it has little importance. In the east we had the fishing industry centred on Grimsby, but it had little in common with farming except some weather lore. The coastal areas, including Grimsby, had some distinctive dialectal usages of their own, e.g. **howry** weather for persistent light rain, and the sandbanks out on the flat beaches are still referred to as **binks**.

The retention of old forms in the dialects meant that the labourer usually expressed himself in words from Old English roots. These were short and concise as opposed to the longer Latin-based words favoured by scholars. He would **make** rather than 'construct'. **get** and not 'obtain', **pump up** a tyre and not 'inflate' it, and **look into** a situation but not 'investigate' it.

The dialectal pronunciations of words were often survivals that differed from present day English as in:-

"I went round be the road",

where **be** is a weak form of 'by'. The Oxford English Dictionary says that **be** is 'uniform in northern dialects since the Middle English period'. In writings of the age we find many examples of the **be** spelling to represent the pronunciation of that time, as in *Mandeville's Travels* (c.1400):-

'And right as the pearl taketh roundness, right so the diamond be virtu of God taketh squareness.',

and again in *Ceix and Alceone* by John Gower (d. 1408):-

'As he which wolde go be schipe.' (ship)

and

'Which slepe schal be nyhte.'
(Which shall sleep by night.)

In his *Adrian and Bardus* we find:-

'And made his covenant be mouthe.'

The dialectal use of **snewed** for 'snowed' is found in Chaucer's *Prologue to The Canterbury Tales*:-

'It snewed in his hous.'

Many of our dialectal variations from standard English appear to be uninformed, but before we dismiss them as such it might be as well to investigate the reasons for their existence. In some cases it is English and not the dialect that is the deviant.

III

PRONUNCIATIONS IN LINCOLNSHIRE DIALECTS

The greatest divergence between the dialects of the different regions is in the vowel sounds. Even in one area these are very fluid and it is difficult to find any rules other than local usage. Sometimes vowels are interchanged for no apparent reason. It is common to hear children sing in school,

> 'May they be, like Josiph, loving,
> Dutiful, and chaste, and pure;
> And their faith, like Daved, proving,
> Steadfast unto death endure.'

Frequent correction of this verse is necessary, for they usually revert to the dialect vowels the next time the hymn is sung. Vowel sounds are so flexible in the dialects that they must be regarded as tendencies rather than as fixed rules. This is not confined to Lincolnshire dialect speakers. Even on the radio we hear pronunciations like rhodedendron, Can**i**da and childr**un**.

In Lincolnshire the **a** sound is usually short as in 'matter'. so that 'bath', 'dance' and 'lather' are crisper than the southern **bahth, dahnce** and **lahther**. The latter pronunciations would have sounded strange to our dialect speakers, and if any local person dared to use them they would have been ridiculed for putting on airs and 'talking fine'. This shortening can go so far as to reduce the **a** to an **e**, 'had' becoming **hed**; 'wash' **wesh**; 'grass', **gress**; and 'sacks'; **secks**. 'Make' and 'master' in the west of the county were **mek** and **mester**, but in the Marshes the vowels were more often extended to **maäke** and **maäster**. When an **a** has an **o** sound as in 'what' in standard English this is ignored in the dialect, and words are pronounced as they are spelt with a short **a**, unlike RP which has changed to **o** after the **w**, so we say wh**a**t, w**a**nder, w**a**nt, w**a**tch, sw**a**llow, squ**a**t and qu**a**lify. If an **a** is followed by an **r** it is sounded as in 'far'. so we get sw**arm**, w**ar**, w**arm**, w**arn**, qu**art** and qu**ar**ter. These follow the rule in standard English words like 'marmalade', 'cart' and 'margarine', but in many cases English deviates when it gives words like 'warm' a **wawm** sound. The long **a** in words like 'lake' and 'same' is usually further extended to **laäke** and **saäme**. This is one of the stronger tendencies of the east Lincolnshire dialects, so that it can almost be regarded as a rule. giving us **aäble, aäcre, haäfe** (half). **maäde, maäte, raäke, saäge, taäpe, taäste**, etc. There are a few exceptions as where 'chain' becomes **cheeän**, 'strain', **streeän** and 'drain' **dreeän**. 'Straight' is often pronounced **stright** as in Mabel Peacock's *Th' Lincolnsheer Poächer*,

'A narrer, rough roäd to heaven,
And a stright, smoothe waäy to hell.'

Conversely, 'right' is usually **reight.**

Where an **e** sound is spelt **ea** as in 'feather', 'wealth', 'ready', 'weather' and 'steady' the standard English pronunciation is used, but 'death', 'bread', 'lead' (the metal) and 'sweat' were in the east of the county normally pronounced as **deäth, breäd, leäd** and **sweät**, thus not undergoing the change of RP and have stayed the same pronunciation as other words of their group, such as **reäd**, **beät** and **deäd**. Generally words spelt with **ee** are kept distinct and 'reed', 'beet' and 'deed' have the same pronunciation as in RP. 'Great' too has kept with its traditional group in the east of the county as **greät,** but on the western side of Lincolnshire it tends to be **gret**. 'Earn', 'learn' and 'concern' were dialectally **arn**, **larn**, and **consarn**. When a word contained **ei** or **ey** the change was normally to **aä** as in **thaäy** and **naäither.** The double **e** is still sometimes extended to **eä** as in 'reäl'. Tennyson gives it in *Northern Style*, *Old Style*, when he writes of a 'boggle' or ghost of a gamekeeper.

'Keäper's it wur; fo' they fun 'um theer a-laid of 'is faäce
Down i' the woild enemies.' (anemones).

'Spread' is usually pronounced as **spreed.**

When **i** precedes **gh** as in 'fight' it changes to **feight**, as does 'right' to **reight**, but in the north-west of the county, particularly in the Isle of Axholme, it takes on a double **e** sound as in **leet** for 'light'. **neet** for 'night', **seet** for 'sight' and **breet** for 'bright'. Mabel Peacock. who wrote in the dialect of Kirton Lindsey, about 1890 in her *Lincolnsheer Poächer*, tells of

'Wheare rabbits cum oot on' play,
An' stamp wi' the'r feet o' a moonleet neet'.

The long **o** as in 'road', 'home', 'bone', and 'hope' is extended to **roäd, hoäme, boäne,** and **hoäpe.** 'So' becomes **soä**, not very far removed from the Old English **swa**. The north-west county pronunciation of **ow** is frequently **oo** in words like **coo** (cow), **croon** (crown), and **broon** (brown), and in the same area a 'plough' is a **ploo**. In the rest of the county **ow** sometimes becomes **aw** as in words like **craw** (crow), **graw** (grow), **knaw** (know), **raw** (row of houses), **slaw** (slow), and **snaw** (snow). This had a certain validity, for we read in *Sir Gawayne and the Grene Knight* (c. 1350-75),

'The quyte snaw lay besyde.'
('The white snow lay beside.')

'Thaw', however, is pronounced **thow**, to rhyme with 'know'. Occasionally the long **o** takes on an **eä** sound, as when 'won't' becomes **weänt.**

Occasionally an initial long **o** is shortened so that 'over' becomes **ovver** and 'open' is pronounced as **oppen.** An elderly Lincolnshire man married a young wife, but the union was not a success. He bemoaned his fate to a friend who asked, "Why did you marry such a young lass?" His rueful reply was, "Well, I wanted somebody to cloäse my eyes, but she's oppened 'em!"

U retains everywhere the older Chaucerian pronunciation as in 'bull'. This is in contrast to the southern English **u** that often approximates to an **a**, so that it is difficult to decide when a Cockney says, "You wanna rab it" whether you want **a rabbit** or **to rub** it.

Tch at the end of a word is often given the Scandinavian pronunciation of **k**, so that 'thatch' is **thak**, 'flitch' is **flik**, 'pitch' **pik,** and a 'pitch-fork' a **pik-ferk**. This has a Middle English ancestry. In *The Towneley Play of Noah* (c. 1475) God tells the old patriarch to,

'Anoint thi ship with pik and tar, without and als within'.

The final **-dge** is curtailed in **brig** (bridge) and **rig** (ridge), another Scandinavian influence. Note that in standard English 'sledge' is often cut to 'sled'.

'Rough', 'through', 'though', 'plough' and 'thought' all have different sounds for **ough**, but in dialect some of them besides 'rough' retain the former **uff** pronunciation. My grandfather always said **thruff** for 'through', and his 'though' was **thuff**. A 'plough' was a **plow** unless he became annoyed, and then it was a b...... **pluff**. 'Straight through' was **slap thruff** or **slick thruff**, and Tennyson uses this in his *Owd Roä*,

' . . . But it's down, an' all on it now
Goän into mangles an' tonups, an' raäved slick thruff by the plow.'

In Richard of Hampole's *Love is Life* (c. 1400) we find,

'Thof us thynk the way be dregh,'
(Though we think the way is drear.)

and again,

'Thof he wer neuer sa wylde,'
(Though he was never so wild,)

A strong characteristic of Lincolnshire speech is the retroflex R. This is a full-blooded R produced by curling up the tongue with the tip almost touching the roof of the mouth. Farm is pronounced as **faRm** rather than **fahm**, and there is **theeäRe**, not **theya** as in standard English where the **r** is softened till it is almost lost.

The glottal stop is used in some parts of the county, but not in others. It is produced by closing the glottis and compressing air behind it in the lungs. Then the glottis is opened rapidly so that the air escapes suddenly, producing a sound rather like an extremely light cough. It is used dialectically in some words where **t** is the norm in standard English. As phonetic symbols are not being used in this booklet the glottal stop is indicated by a dash, so that in dialect 'butter' is **bu-er** and 'water' is **wa-er.** A Mid-Lincolnshire man when asked where he was going might answer, "I'm o'-gi- a bi- o' bu-er." (I'm off to get a bit of butter), or one might hear, "Wha- a lo- o' li-le bo-les " (What a lot of little bottles). This is not found in all parts of the county. In the north 'water' is **watter,** the **t** being sounded and the **a** short, but in central Lincolnshire the glottal stop is strong and we say **wa-er,** the **a** being short again. However, further south around Boston, it becomes nearer to **worter,** and the glottal stop disappears, only to come in again further south when the Cockney says **waw-a.**

Some Lincolnshire words are different from the standard English versions in that they have certain letters transposed. This is known as 'metathesis'. 'Lorry' becomes **rully** (though only in the case of the horse-drawn vehicle), and '-thorpe' at the end of a place-name is often **-throp, -trop,** or **-trup,** 'Grainthorpe' being **Grantrup** and 'Aisthorpe' **Aistrop.** 'Burgh le Marsh' is pronounced **Borough,** but 'Burgh on Bain' with the same spelling is metathesised to **Bruff.** 'Venomous', 'stallion', 'starling', 'ask', 'pattern', and 'burst' in the dialect of Mid-Lincolnshire become **vemonous, stanniel, starnil, aks, pattren,** and **brust.** These forms, commonly found in Chaucer and other fourteenth Century writers, may still be heard today among old folk in the villages of Lincolnshire.

IV
CHARACTERISTICS OF THE DIALECTS

The dialectal forms of words vary according to geographical areas, the social standing of the speaker, and how stress is applied to give emphasis to what is said. It is in the attainment of emphasis that dialect is much less rigid and far more subtle than standard English.

The division of Lincolnshire into four main dialectal regions has already been defined in the section on The Validity of the Dialect, but occasionally geographical conditions cut right across the neat arrangements we devise. The word **howry** is interesting. It means miserable, drizzly weather if someone says, "It's howry" but it is applied also to anything of which one does not approve, and is used to indicate disgust. Tennyson's Village Wife says of the late Squire,

"But I 'ears es e'd gie fur a howry owd book thutty pound an' moor.' The word is from the old Danish **haar**, the mist that comes inland off the sea at the time of high tides, now usually known as **sea haar**. Obviously this is a coastal word. It is found in various forms like **owery**, **howry** and **haary** right up the east coast from The Wash to Scotland. In Grantham, only thirty miles inland, the word is almost unknown.

Social standing in the community also determined how words should be pronounced. The farmer's wife who dare not do something might say, "I dursn't" which was considered much more sophisticated than the labourer's, "I dossn't." Telling a child not to do something, the labourer's wife might shout, "Gi' ower" but the lady of the farm would say, "Give hoäver." These differences do not seem very important to us, but they were considered to be the hallmark of one's place in society and everybody knew his place. They firmly believed that

'The rich man in his castle,
The poor man at his gate,
God made them high or lowly
And ordered their estate.'

Those who talked 'posh' were quickly derided into reverting to their natural speech, not only by their 'betters' but by their equals who considered that they were acting above their stations.

It is in the field of emphasis that dialect comes to its own. Where standard English relies on intonation, inflexion, and stress, dialect uses other devices to give wider and more subtle variations. The shortening of the vowel is common. In the word 'take' the **a** is normally extended to **taäke**, so that a child may be told, "**Taäke** this to yer muther." A person being teased by someone placing an obstruction in his path could become angry and say, "Tek it awäy!" **Gaming** is not gambling, but playing in Lincolnshire. If asked where the children are a person might reply, "Gaämin' i' the laäne" but if a child who had been set to do a job of work started playing about he could be told to "Git on wi' it an' stop gammin' about!" This clipping of a normally extended vowel gives a word much more emphasis.

A change of vowel is employed for the same purpose in the word 'you'. In the dialect it is usually shortened to **ya** as in "Can I come wi' ya?" If someone tells an incredulous tale that requires proof he may be challenged with "How do **yah** knaw?", an increase in emphasis, but even more is attained by a change to **yow**. "Yow are a lumpheäd!" may be said in disgust to a person considered to be acting foolishly.

The terminal **a** was frequently encountered, but it has almost died out now. In Tennyson's *Northern Farmer, Old Style* the old man says of Bessie Marris who once bore a child that might have been his,

'Mowt a beän mayhap, for she wur a bad 'un, sheä'

There is nothing inconsistent in the use of both she and **sheä** in this line. The latter is for emphasis and would have been spoken with some venom. The terminal **a** was very much in evidence in my childhood at Methodist Prayer Meetings after evening services. Old gentlemen in the congregation would offer their individual prayers, slowly and with great emphasis like, "O Lord**a**, we thank**a** Thee that once again**a** we are permitted**a** to approach**a** Thy thron**a** . . etc." The normal cry to call the cows home in Lincolnshire was "Cush! cush!" This was adequate in parts of the county where fields were enclosed by hedges or ditches, but in the more open Fens where cattle could be more widely dispersed "Cusha cusha " was used, the **a** adding emphasis so that the call carried farther. Jean Ingelow records this in her *High Tide on the Coast of Lincolnshire.*

Lincolnshire people are often accused by outsiders of dropping their h's or using them in the wrong places. From the viewpoint of the pedant this is true, though Chaucer usually used **hit** for it, and in Richard Rolle of Hampole's *Love is Life* (c. 1400) one line runs,

'Of lufe sal he na thyng tyne that hit in hert will halde.'
(Of love shall he nothing lose that it in heart will hold.)

Hit in Middle English was a correct development, but the **h** has now been lost in standard English though it is retained in some northern dialects, particularly in Northumberland.

It must be pointed out that there are rules other than those of English grammar, and for the uninitiated to condemn these is rather like a soccer enthusiast shouting, "Hands " at a Rugby match. Usually the aspirate is omitted, so we hear **'arvest**, **'ouse**, **'inder,** and **'umbug**. Though this is considered slovenly it is normal standard English in 'honest', where to sound the **h** would brand the speaker as uneducated, and many people drop the **h** in 'hotel'. Words like 'what', 'when', 'whether' and 'which' begin with a **wh** spelling, but we pronounce it as **hw**, and indeed, that is how they were originally spelt in the Old English. If this initial aspirate is sounded in normal speech today it usually indicates that the speaker comes from the Midlands or farther north as the southerner frequently drops the **h** and says **wat, wen, wether** and **wich**.

The Lincolnshire **h** is reserved for special purposes. The educated speaker emphasises a word by giving it a special intonation or pronunciation, but the Lincolnshire dialect speaker uses an initial aspirate to emphasise a word, e.g. "Hi wouldn't do that!" The farmer in Tennyson's *Owd Roä*, describing a fire that destroyed the family home says,

". . . but it's all ower now - hall hower - an' ten year sin'."

The aspirated second **hall hower** emphasises the first one. Again, in the poet's *Churchwarden and the Curate* the old man declares,

"An' saw by the Graäce o' the Lord, Mr. Harry,
I ham what I ham"

This is said with far more emphatic satisfaction than

"I am what I am!"

The articles 'an' and 'the(e)' (pronounced 'thee') are used in Standard English before a vowel. In Lincolnshire it is common practice to employ 'a' and 'the' almost always, even when the next word begins with a vowel, but **a** apple, **a** egg, **a** iron, **the** orange and **the** umbrella do not flow readily off the tongue. The difficulty is overcome by using an **h** to improve the fluency, so we say a **ha**pple, **a hi**ron, the **ho**range and the **hu**mbrella' This function of the aspirate is entirely divorced from standard English usage. Though the article 'the(e)' is rare it did find a function in country Methodist chapels, not to be used when the following word began with a vowel, but to give emphasis to hymns much as the terminal **a** did to prayers. Frequently we could hear "**The(e)** head that once was crowned with thorns", "**The(e)** King of Love my Shepherd is" and "When I survey **the(e)** wondrous cross." The **h** was used almost anywhere or omitted in names of persons and places. 'Horncastle' would be either **Hurnc'sle** or **Urnc'sle,** 'Authorpe' **Hautherp** or **Autherp,** and 'Harry', unless spoken emphatically, would be **'Arry.**

The double negative is used widely in the county to emphasise a statement. Under the pressure of grammarians schooled in Latin grammar this is considered incorrect, but it was consistently used in Old and Middle English.

Robert Mannyng, in his *Dancers of Colbeck* (c. 1375) writes:

'Noght yn none holy stedes.'
(Not in no holy places.)

Though it has been expelled from good literary style the double negative still survives in dialect. Tennyson used it in his *Northern Farmer, Old Style*,

'I moän't a 'naw moor aäle',

in *The Village Wife*,

' 'E dosn' not coom fro' the shere',

and

' 'E niver not fished 'is awn ponds,'

Robert Lowth, in his *Short Introduction to English Grammar* (1762) formulated the rule that 'Two negatives in English destroy one another, or are equivalent to an affirmative.' His mathematical thinking applied to English grammar destroyed a valid and previously accepted means of expressing emphasis. Our language is poorer for it.

Words ending in **-ly** were sometimes emphasised by lengthening the last syllable, so that 'surely' became **sewer-lye** and 'accordingly' was **according-lye**.

The **d - th** interchange (as in the Welsh Pontypridd, pronounced 'Pontypreeth') is an old survival in Lincolnshire. In the works of fourteenth century writers it works both ways, 'mother' being written as **moder** and 'could' as **couthe**. In Chaucer's *Sompnoures Tale* we read,

' 'Pees', quod our host, for Cristes moder deere'.'
('Peace , quoth our host, 'for Christ's mother dear'.)

and in *Sir Gawayne and the Grene Knight* (c. 1350-75),

'He couthe hit not deme with spelle.'
(He could it not judge with speaking, i.e. He could not say which it was.)

This interchange is found in the dialect words **fother** (fodder), **lether** (ladder), **consither** (consider), **farden** (farthing) and **pad** (path). A blacksmith's anvil is both a **stiddy** and a **stithy** in Lincolnshire. Louth takes its name from the River Lud, and it is interesting to note that while the river retained the old **d** sound the town took on the **th** to **Luth** and later to 'Louth'.

The plural of 'that' is not usually 'those', but **them** is heard as in

"I like them apples",

and

"When thaäy stop layin' I shall kill them 'ens."

Some English words have an **au** sound that is written as **al** as in 'stalk', 'walk', 'talk' and 'chalk'. The pronunciation is changed in 'calf', but the dialect speaker renders it as **cauf** according to the general pattern. The rule is observed in place-names where 'Haltham' is Hautam, 'Calceby' Cauceby, 'Walmsgate' Waumsgate, and 'Alvingham' Auvingham, but 'Alford' is pronounced 'Olford'. The **al** is still fluid in 'falcon' which may be **falcon, folcon,** or **faucon** according to the custom of the speaker. Robert Mannyng in *The Dancers of Colbeck* uses **autere** for 'altar',

> 'The preste that stode at the autere.'
> (The priest that stood at the altar.)

The dialectal use of **that there** and **this here** as intensives of identification is considered to be bad English, but many folk who condemn this form of emphasis do not hesitate to use current phrases such as "I myself . . . " and "At this moment of time . . . "

A characteristic of Lincolnshire speech is the pronominal **a**, that is the use of **a** for 'I', 'he', and 'she'. The history of this goes back to the time when the Danes were settling in England and marrying their language to the Anglo-Saxon speech. Otto Jespersen in his *Growth and Structure of the English Language* states,

> 'The most important importation of this kind (from the Scandinavian) was that of the pronominal forms **they, them** and **their**, which entered readily into the system of English pronouns beginning with the same sound (**the, that, this**) and were felt to be more distinct than the old native forms which they supplanted. Indeed these were liable to constant confusion with some forms of the singular number (**he, him, her**) after the vowels had become obscured, so that **he** and **hie, him** and **heom, her** (**hire**) and **heora** could no longer be kept easily apart. We thus find the obscured form, which was written **a** (or 'a), in use for he till the beginning of the sixteenth century (compare the dialectal use, for instance, in Tennyson's 'But Parson a cooms an' a goäs'), and in use for **she** and for **they** till the end of the fourteenth century.'

The reference to the use of **a** for 'he' is from Tennyson's *Northern Farmer, Old Style*.

Though Jespersen says that the pronominal **a** lasted until the beginning of the sixteenth century, it was in use for 'he' by some dialect speakers to within living memory. Far from dying out it survives strongly in the Lincolnshire Marshes today in place of 'I'. so we hear, "A said A would do it", "A want to goä hoäame", and "If A live A shall coom o' Sunday."

There is an affinity betweeen 'on' and 'of' in the county, so that they are frequently used in place of each other, e.g. "She goäs to church of a Sunday," and "Them's good beäst. A'd like to buy some on 'em." A Lincolnshire simile goes, "It's all of a heap, like a bull turd." In Tennyson's *Owd Roä* the farmer was in his chair,

'Wi' Roäver athurt my feeät, an' sleepin still as a stoän
Of a Christmas Eäve.',

and in the same poem he tells of the burnt-out farm,

'All on it goän into mangles and tonups.'

The prefix **a** is used sometimes instead of **be**, so that 'before', 'behind,' 'beside', and 'between' are dialectically **afore, ahind, aside,** and **atwixt**. 'Beneath' does not follow this trend. The word is rarely used, 'underneath' being favoured and usually rendered as **underneän,** though **aneän** occurs sometimes.

The dialects of Lincolnshire have a sound basis, sometimes adhering to the traditional rules of English more closely than standard English itself does, but at other times departing completely from recognised practice. Standard English and dialect can only be studied comparatively, and to apply the rules of either to the other is to fail to understand the true characters of both.

V

LINCOLNSHIRE EXPRESSIONS

Lincolnshire speech is rich in country lore and sayings, many of which are wonderfully expressive, sometimes almost poetic, and often flavoured with a dash of earthy humour.

A child who has freckles is said to have **bran i' the faäce,** or alternatively he's got **turkey eggs.**

Small, fluffy clouds like tufts of cotton wool are called **hen scrattins** (scratchings), and the effect of perspective that gives parallel cloud formations the appearance of an upturned boat stretching across the sky is known as **the ark.**

In the west of the county anyone hearing a braying ass is likely to remark, "There's a tinker dead at Lincoln." A donkey is humorously called a **Jerusalem nightingale**, while croaking frogs (alas, now almost diasppeared, though once heard in their hundreds from over a mile away), were referred to as **Fen nightingales.**

The sounds of horses' hoofs were onomatopoeically described as **butter and eggs, butter and eggs** for a horse at a canter. If the animal happened to be a 'clicker', that is it caught its front hoofs on its rear ones when it was running, there were extra beats in the rhythm and it went **hammer and pinchers, hammer and pinchers,** but a horse at a gallop went **pen and ink, pen and ink.**

Village life was periodically enlivened by evangelical Methodist revival meetings in which eloquent preachers, by verbally shaking them over the pit of Hell, encouraged people to repent and be 'saved'. Outsiders referred to one of these meetings as **a soul do.**

A man far away from his folk and feeling rather homesick might have said. "I wish I had hold of our cat's tail" or "I wish I had hold of our shit-house door."

A countryman would tell his sweetheart that he would marry her 'when the bods (birds) hes two taäils.' This did not mean that he would never marry her, but it was an indirect way of saying that he would marry her in the spring when the swallows came, and it was well understood.

Flour was called **dumplin dust**, and when farmers fed a number of labourers who 'lived in' dumplings were sometimes made so big that the men called them **hoss-leg dumplins.**

The local blacksmith and farrier was much in demand, and the smithy attracted boys who loved to see the bellows force flames from a handful of glowing coals. If he found the smithy becoming too crowded the smith would turn the children out, only to be repaid bv ieers of "Windburner."

In the Isle of Axholme a clothes-horse was called a **winter-hedge** because in that season it was used to dry clothes that in summer would have been spread on the hedges.

Around Boston older people, on seeing seagulls flying towards the coast in the evening, still say, "There's the Fosdyke labourers going home."

The dialectal use of words sometimes gives meanings that differ from those of standard English. The word 'parson' not only means a minister of religion, but it is still used for a black lamb. A black rabbit is also a **parson**, and it was considered very bad luck to shoot one. Indeed, if one did, the luck of the shoot would fade away and the bag at the end of the day would be very small. A guide-post was a **parson** too, so that a lost traveller would want to know, "What does the parson say?" This was Lincolnshire humour. It was called a parson because it points the way but does not take it!

To **hug** not only means to embrace someone but it is more commonly used for 'carry', so that a labourer carrying away sacks of grain when the corn was being threshed would describe his job as **huggin' corn**.

When a fence is being erected a corner post is sometimes given support by a diagonal strut that is secured near the top at an angle of about forty-five degrees, the bottom end being dug into the ground abour three or four feet from the base of the main post. In Lincolnshire this strut is a **godfather**, and **strut** is the name given to a stickleback.

A person suffering from ill-health might describe himself as feeling **mean**. I remember a vicar, who, interpreting the word as meaning 'stingy', used to delight in asking an old man how he was just to hear the unvarying reply, "I'm mean, sir, I'm mean."

Someone in a bad temper was said to be **ugly**. The labourer, when asked how his wife was and replied, "She was rare and ugly this mornin", was not informing the enquirer that her beauty had declined. If she had heard him she would not have taken it as an insult, but as a simple statement that they had exchanged a few harsh words before he went to work.

If someone considered to be of no particular importance acted as if he were of some consequence he was said to be **as big as bull beef**. This did not refer to the size of the animal, but to the coarseness of the grain in meat from an old bull.

Misers were sometimes reminded that, "Ya can't taäke it wi' ya. Theere's noä pockets in a shroud!"

A really keen knife was said to be so sharp you could "carve a flea's eye wi' it", but a very blunt one was dismissed with "I could ride bare-arsed to London on it!"

Children being warned that it was their bed-time were told, "It's time you went up the wooden hill" (stairs), or "You'll be late for Lily White's party" (a reference to lily-white sheets).

An idle person was told that he was as lazy as Ludlum's dog, and he leaned against the doorpost to bark!

Four different degrees of intoxication were recognised, **sheep drunk** when a man became merry and easily handled, **lion drunk** when he was brave and boastful, **ape drunk** when he got up to silly, irresponsible tricks, and **sow drunk** when he fell to the ground in an alcoholic stupor. Hence the saying, "As drunk as David's sow."

People said of those they considered unintelligent, "He doesn't know a B from a bull's foot."

The word **throng**, meaning busy, was used in the north of the county as it was in Yorkshire, but it is rarely heard in other parts of Lincolnshire. The simile most encountered was, "As throng as Throp's wife when she hinged hersen (hanged herself) wi' a dish-clout" (dish-cloth).

The usual exclamation of amazement was, "Laws-a-massy-me!", a corruption of "Lord have mercy upon me!"

Obviously this collection of sayings does not claim to be complete, but it serves to illustrate how our forebears expressed their thoughts about the situations they encountered in simple day-to-day living.

VI

MIDDLE ENGLISH SURVIVALS IN DIALECT

There is a scarcity of writings in Old English because comparatively little was penned, and most of what was written has not survived. A certain amount of our Lincolnshire speech can be traced back to this period and we can conjecture about much more, but a great deal of Old English may have survived in the dialect for which we can produce no proof because there is lack of written evidence.

Middle English writers have left us manuscripts that are not only greater in number than Old English survivals, but are written in the patois of different regions, giving us some idea of the dialectal distribution of the period. Spelling was a matter of individual taste within certain limits. Often the value allotted to a letter in Latin was widely known and if local pronunciation varied so might the spelling, but there were no dictionaries to consult to find the 'correct' spelling of a word. It is important to bear in mind that variations in spelling do not necessarily mean that pronunciations are different. Conversely, differing pronunciations may be written with identical spellings. Many of the surviving manuscripts are not originals, but copies made by scriveners. Some were paid according to the number of the lines they copied, and the tendency was to use the longer of alternative spellings to increase their output and pay. Not all copyists were meticulous in their work. Chaucer had to reprimand his scrivener, Adam, for carelessness,

> 'But after my makyng thou wryte more trewe,
> So ofte a-daye I mot thy werk renewe,
> It to correcte and eek to rubbe and scrape,
> And al is through thy negligence and rape.'

Bearing all these factors in mind, there is still considerable evidence that many Middle English words, pronunciations, and usages, now considered obsolescent as far as standard English is concerned, have survived in the dialects of Lincolnshire. A short list is given as evidence of this. For each word an example of dialectal usage is presented followed by a quotation from a Middle English writer. To avoid needless repetition a list of works quoted is given, together with relevant dates:-

1. *Sir Orfeo*. Anon. 1325-1350.
2. *The Taking of Calais*. Laurence Minot. 1347.
3. *Love is Life* and *Seven Gifts of the Holy Ghost*. Richard Rolle of Hampole. Died 1349.
   Sir Gawayne and the Grene Knight. Anon. 1350-1375.

5. Chaucer. 1340-1400.
6. *The Gest Hystoriale of the Destruction of Troy*. Anon. c. 1375
7. *Piers Plowman*. William Langland. 1362-1400.
8. John of Trevisa's Translation of *Higden's Polychronicon*. c. 1352.
9. *Ceix and Alceone*. John Gower. Died 1408.
10. *Mandeville's Travels*. From Cotton MS. Titus C xvi. c. 1400-25.
11. York Play of *The Harrowing of Hell*. Anon. c. 1430-40.
12. The Towneley Play of *Noah*. Anon. c. 1475.

AYTHER. Either.
"Ayther on (of) 'em will do."
Towneley Play of *Noah:* 'Ayther bi northe or southe.'
Sir Gawayne and the Grene Knight: 'Hit had an hole on the end and on ayther side.'

BEES. Is.
"Theere he bees "
Richard Rolle, *Love is Life:*
'Swylk es this worlde, I wene and bees till Domesdaye.'
(Such is this world, I think, and is till Domesday.)

BREED. Breadth or width.
Invited to help one's self to cake at table a person might be told, "Doän't be scared to cut yersen (yourself) a good breed."
Towneley Play of *Noah:*
'Lo, here the lenght,
Thre hundreth cubettis euenly;
Of breed, lo, it is fyfty.'

BRIG. Bridge.
"The floods weshed the brig awaäy last night."
Sir Gawayne and the Grene Knight:
'The brygge was brayde doun.'
(The bridge was lowered down.)

BYCAUSE. (Pronounced bye-cause) Because.
"The family caäme hoäme last Sunday bycause o' the Christenin."
Tennyson's *Northern Farmer, New Style:*
'Couldn' I luvv thy muther by cause o' 'er munny laäid by?'

CHAUMBER. Chamber.
"The Waggoners chaumber is ower the kitchen."
Tennyson's *Owd Roä:*
'Thou slep i' the chaumber above us.'
Sir Orfeo:
'He come with knightes tene (ten)
To chaumber right before the queen.'

DOWTER. (ow as in 'mow') Daughter.
"My dowter left school last week."
Ceix and Alceone:
'Many a dowhter and a sone.'

DWINE. Dwine away. To waste away.
"She was in a decline (suffered from tuberculosis) and she just seemed to dwine away."
Sir Orfeo:
'Al his bodi was away duine.'

DING. A blow struck, usually at someone.
"If ya doän't behaäve I'll gi' ya a greät ding i' the 'eäd."
Piers Plowman:
'Diken, or deluen, or dyngen vppon sheues.'
(Ditching, or digging, or dinging upon sheaves, i.e. threshing.)

FUN. Found.
A short vowel is sometimes used in Lincolnshire before **nd** and the last of these two letters is omitted, so that 'pound' becomes **pun** as in 'a five pun noäte'.
"I fun a straäy dog i' my yard."
The Towneley Play of *Noah:*
'As peradventure may be fun.'

GAINSAY. To speak against or contradict.
"Doän't gainsay me when I tell ya the truth "
Richard Rolle, *Seven Gifts of the Holy Ghost:*
'Peté es that a man be mylde and gaynesay noghte Haly Writte.'
(Piety is that a man be gentle and gainsay not Holy Writ.)

GRESS. Grass.
"Yah'll catch cowd if ya sit o' that wet gress."
Sir Gawayne and the Grene Knight:
'. . . and overgrown with gresse.'

HERONSEWS. Herons.
"The owd heronsews was caällin' out 'Frank! Frank!' across the marsh."
Because of their cry herons are sometimes called 'Frankies' in Lincolnshire.
Chaucer, *The Squire's Tale:*
"I wol nat tellen of her straunge sewes,
Ne of her swannes, ne here herounsewes,'
(I will not tell of her strange pursuits,
Nor of her swans, nor her herons.)

LIG. Lie.
"Are ya goin 'to lig i' bed till dinner time?"
Sir Orfeo:
'But let her lig and rest take.'

Note that **lig** is not usually employed to mean 'lie' as an untruth, but a liar is frequently called a **ligger.** This is a kind of dialect pun; it is not considered strong language and may be accepted in a spirit of fun. To call a man a liar would invite retaliation.

LOW.

Flame. Usually **lally-low** in Lincolnshire.
"I likes to pull up to the lally-low."
(I like to pull my chair near to the fire.)
The Destruction of Troy (c. 1375):
'They were brent on the buerne with the breme low.'
(They were burnt on the sea by the fierce flame.)

MAÄSTER. Master. The extended **a** is used in the Lincolnshire Marshes.

Caller, to woman who has answered the door: "Is the maäster in?"
Woman: "Yes, I'm here "
Chaucer, *The Cokes Tale:*
'This jolly prentys with his mayster bood.'
(This jolly apprentice with his master abode.)

NOBBUT. Nothing but.

"He's nobbut a bairn "
Sir Gawayne and the Grene Knight:
'And al was holy inwith, nobot an olde caue.'
(And all was hollow within, nothing but an old cave.)

PENS. Feathers.

When a chicken was hand plucked sometimes small, developing feathers were left in the skin. Dialectically these were called **pens,** and they had to be removed by trapping them between the thumb and the blade of a knife to pull them out. This was known as **penning** the chicken.
Mandeville's Travels refers to the gryphon:
'And of hire ribbes, and of the pennes of hire wenges (wings) men maken bowes full stronge.'

PICK. Pitch.

"The best cure for piles is pick pills."
This was an old country remedy.
The Towneley Play of *Noah,* describing the ark:
'Pyk and tar full sure thereupon laid.'

PIKE. Look, peep.

"I saw her pike at the woman next door."
Chaucer, *Troilus and Creseyde:*
'Come neer and gan in at the curtin pike.'
(Came near and did in at the curtain peep.)

RIG. Back. The beam that runs along the ridge of a roof, forming the back-bone, is called the **rigtree.**

Tennyson's *Owd Roä* tells of help arriving too late to prevent the farm house being destroyed by fire:
'Haäfe o' the parish runn'd oop when the rigtree was tummlin' in.'
Sir Orfeo:
'And heng his harp his rig upon.'
(And hung his harp upon his back.)

SLOCKEN. To put out a fire.

"Slocken that fire afore ya come to bed."
Richard Rolle, *Love is Life:*
'Lüfe I lyke till a fyre that slocken may na thyng.'
(Love I liken to a fire that nothing may put out.)

SPREED. Spread.

"I like to spreed my butter thick soä as I can taäste it."
Sir Orfeo:
'To se the floures sprede and spring.'
(To see the flowers spread and spring.)

TENT. To look after, or take care of.

As children we used to **tent** cattle grazing on the grass verges of the roads.
The Harrowing of Hell:
'Tane for to tent.'
In the Towneley Play of *Noah* the patriarch tells his wife to,
'Tent the stere-tre.'
(Look after the steer-tree, or helm.)

WAP. A blow or stroke .(Short **a** to rhyme with **nap.**)

On the old self-binder that cut the corn and tied it into sheaves there were lengths of stout lath that beat the standing crop towards the knives and then on to a moving canvas. These were called 'waps'.
Sir Gawayne and the Grene Knight:
'When thou wypped of my hede at a wap one.'
(When you whipped off my head at one stroke.)

VII

DISAPPEARING DIALECT

Little is left of the real Lincolnshire dialects. They are disappearing faster then is sometimes realised because the accents that remain are often regarded as dialects. Accents are just one part of the local patois that also consist of vocabulary, intonations, idioms, and all the subtle variations that separate them from other dialects. It cannot be too strongly emphasised that English spoken with a regional accent only is not a complete dialect, and we must be careful to distinguish between the two.

The old dialect-speaking local preacher who read the Scriptures from the pulpit was using his local accent. Neither the words nor the idiom were dialectal, but belonged to Biblical English. The story of the raising of Lazarus as recorded in St. John XI, 1 - 46, includes the words,

'He cried with a loud voice, Lazarus, come forth. And he that was dead came forth, bound hand and foot with grave-clothes.'
This would be read by the preacher as,

"E cried wi' a lowd voice, Lazarus, cum ferth. An' 'e that was deäd caäme ferth, bound 'and and fut wi' graäve-cloaäs.'
But this is not dialect. No Lincolnshire man would say naturally, 'he cried with a loud voice' or 'come forth.' The idiom is wrong. He would be much more likely to say,

"E shouted, Lazarus, cum yah 'ere. An' 'im as wos deäd comed out, lapped hall hower wi' clouts.'*

Many modern dialect writers use the regional pronunciations but ignore the local syntax and idioms. They think in English and overlay their thoughts with an accent, calling it dialect. To write good dialect one must think in dialect, and to do this it must have been lived and experienced. Dialect writing is subjective and rarely sounds authentic if it is written objectively. In describing how one rejected proffered advice, someone might say "I didn't listen to any of them", and transposing it into dialect they could produce, "I didn't listen to ony on 'em." Tennyson, faced with the same situation in *The Spinster's Sweet'arts* writes, 'I niver not listened to noän'. This has a feeling of authenticity about it, redundant negatives and all. Would-be dialect writers face the greatest of difficulties because if they write good dialect it could be too 'broad' to be understood in a world where the local forms of speech have almost gone. If they write a diluted form in order to be understood it ceases to be good dialect. Most modern writers produce better dialect prose than they do verse. Those who

* Wyclif (c. 1320-1384) gives it as 'lapped in cloutes'

know the idiom and can use it correctly sometimes find difficulty when they try to make lines scan, often reverting to standard English in order to do so, to the detriment of the dialect. The danger is that much of the pseudodialect written today may be accepted in the future as authentic.

Tennyson has been much quoted in these pages. His dialect poems, even in his lifetime, were considered laborious to read and not easy to understand, so until recently they have been somewhat neglected. The difficulty was that those who spoke the dialect were usually not good readers, and those who read fluently rarely spoke the dialect well. His Lincolnshire verses are not only brilliant character monologues that are very rewarding reading as poetry, but they are also by far the best of our county dialect readings. It is not enough to use the right words. They must be arranged in syntax and idiom that differs from normal English usage, and he knew how to do this. Tennyson, in an unhappy childhood, spent much of his time among the labourers around Somersby, absorbing their speech so that he was able to reproduce it right to the end of his life. He was so familiar with it that he was able to use words in different dialectal forms (e.g. half is given in different poems as **aäf, hafe** and **haäfe,)** but he took great pains to check his dialect with people who could verify what he had written.

As time passes many of the old Lincolnshire words disappear. Some of them are not greatly missed because they left behind standard English synonyms. There were others, however, that had delicate shades of meaning and their passing is to be regretted, e.g. **abless** and **spang.**

Here is a selection of words commonly used in my childhood that are rarely heard today :–

AÄME. Condensation on a window.

"I hed to wipe the aäme off the winders afore I could see out."

ABLESS. Able-less, helpless.

Sometimes used to describe a person who is old and losing his faculties. It usually has a more subtle connotation in that it is applied to someone who is incompetent to manage his money so that he is permanently in debt. Such a person is not a spendthrift, but is making a genuine but unsuccessful effort to control his finances.

ABLINS. Perhaps.

"Ablins the lambin' will start next week."

ABOON. Above. (Used mainly in north-west Lincolnshire.)

"The bad 'arvist 'es browt prices aboon what us poor foälks can paäy."

AG. Sometimes HAG. To cut something in a careless or clumsy manner.

"Doän't ag that meät like that or it weän't be fit ta yet". (eat)

AGAÄTE. Started.

"Git agaäte o' diggin' or ya weän't finish afore supper."

ANEAN. Beneath.

"That hen's goän broody soä I'll put a sittin' o' eggs aneän 'er."

ANEW. Enough.

"Tek it eäsy, theere's time anew afore night."

AÄISE. To throw away, particularly a liquid like dirty water.

"Doän't leäve that watter theere, aäise it ower the wall."

ARSE-END-UP. Upside down.

"'E slithered and landed arse-end-up i' the squad."

ARSE-FOST. (first) Back to front.

"I knaw as 'e can't read fer 'e looks at a boök arse-fost.

ATHURT. Athwart, across.

". . . one night I wur sitting' aloan,
Wi' Roäver athurt my feeät, an' sleeäpin' still as a stoän."
Owd Roä, Tennyson.

BACK END. (of the year.) Autumn.

"It's been a rare back end, but theere's sum weather to come."

BATTLE-TWIG. Earwig.

"If battle-twigs gits i' yer ear 'oles thaäy maäkes nests i' yer 'eäd an' yets (eats) yer braäins awaäy."

BEEZUM. An old hag.

Beezum Bet was a character in many of the versions of the Lincolnshire Plough Jags Plays.

"I wish the interferin' owd beezum would goä awaäy."

BELLY-TIMBER. Food.

"Ya want plenty o' belly-timber inside ya if ya want to work this cowd weather."

BING. Bin. A large rat-proof box to contain corn.

"Git a scoop o' corn out o' the bing and feed them 'ens."

BLAÄTE. Bleat.

"The sheep started to blaäte as soon as thaäy saw the dog."

BLIND MAN'S HOLIDAY. Twilight. (See DARKLINS.)

"It's blind man's holiday, soä ya'd better light the candle."

BLOB. To catch eels with a ball of worsted and worms.

An inverted open umbrella is hung just above the surface of the stream, and close alongside it a line is dangled in the water. No hook is used, but on the end of the line is a bunch of worms that have been threaded on worsted. When eels try to take the worms their teeth catch in the worsted and are held long enough for them to be lifted from the water into the umbrella.

"Mam wants a feed o' eels, soä I shall hev to goä and blob fer some."

BOÄK. To retch as if about to vomit.

"I'm sick o' mutton. I've yetten soä much I could boäk at it "

BOÄN-FIRE. Bonfire. Originally this was 'bone-fire', bones being the main material burnt.

"Saäve that rubbish to bon on Boän-fire Night."

BRAÄDES OF. To be like another in appearance or character.

"That bairn braädes of 'is faäther."

BREÄR. Long grass on the verges of roads cut to make hay.

"Theere's breär anew i' the laäne to feed my dunkey fer haäfe a year."

BRIMMING. Said of a sow in season.

"Th'owd sow's brimmin' ageän. I shall ha' to tek 'er to the boär."

BRUSSEN. Burst (Metathesised BURSTEN.)

"The bag was brussen and let the corn run all ower the floor."

BURN DAYLIGHT. To light a lamp or a candle before it was dark enough to make it necessary.

"Blaw that candle out. We can't afford to burn daylight!"

CADDIS. Coloured woollen braids used to decorate the manes and tails of horses.

"We shall ha' to git some new caddis fer the 'osses afore the show."

CAMERILL. A notched stick used to hang up a pig after it had been killed and scraped. The tendons of the rear legs just above the feet were exposed and the camerill pushed through until the notches held the tendons. The carcass was then hauled up by a rope secured to the middle of the camerill.

CAPS OWT. Tops up anything I have ever heard or seen.

"The maäster bowt one o' them tractors what ploughs six furrows at once. It caps owt!"

Variations are CAPS A GARMAN (GERMAN) and CAPS MY ARSE.

CASSONS. Dried cow dung used by the poorest people for fuel in the last century. The practice died out before my time, but I remember the old folk telling me how they gathered cassons in their childhood. This was not popular with the farmers as the fields were being robbed of natural manure.

CAT-LAP. Nonsense.
"'E comed wi' 'is cat-lap about what 'e was goin' to give us, but I shan't voäte fer 'im."

CHAMBER-LEES. Human urine. Formally used by country folk as a fertiliser for onions. Applied neat to lawns it produces a lush, green growth.

CHAPTER FIGURES. Roman numerals, so called because they were used to number the chapters in the Bible.
"Ower clock hes a chapter figure faäce."

CHARMINGS. Paper or rag chewed into small pieces by mice.
"Ya're 'eäd's haäfe full o' nonsense and haäfe full o' mouse charmin's."

CHITTERING. To chatter like birds.
"Th'owd sparrers is chitterin' i' the spoutin's."
"I'm not goin' to the meetin' to listen to a lot o' chitterin' women."
The word also applies to the chattering of teeth.
"She was that cowd her teeth was chitterin'."

CLAM. Thirsty.
"I'm that clam I could sup a gallon."

CON. Know.
"Yah've grown soä big I didn't con ya."

DACKER DOWN. To moderate. Usually applied to weather and speed.
"Theere was a gaäle last night, but it started to dacker down be mornin'."
"Dacker down a bit. I can't keep paäce wi' ya."

DARKLINS. Twilight. Sometimes called BLIND MAN'S HOLIDAY.
"If ya're not hoäme be darklins thaäy'll wonder wheere ya've gotten to."

DINT. Dent.
"Ya'll dint that bucket if ya drop it."

DOÄBLE. Capable of being done. Possible.
"That land's full o' club-root soä ya'll niver grow cabbages on it. It's just not doäble."

DOIT. A half farthing piece, a coin used in the nineteenth century.

"I doän't care a doit fer 'im."

DOOR DARN. A door-post.

"Keep clear o' that door darn. It's just been paäinted."

DYLINGS. Ridges in arable fields, the tops being about eight yards apart to allow drainage along the furrows between, hence the alternative name of RIG AND FURROW cultivation. It was common in Saxon husbandry and was revived at the time of the Corn Laws when wheat was making a high price. Land normally unsuitable for wheat would grow a worth-while crop on the ridges, but when the Corn Laws were repealed this became unprofitable and such land was allowed to revert to pasture. Consequently dylings are sometimes seen in grass fields today. In the south of Lincolnshire they are called DYLANDS.

EYEÄBLE. Pleasant to look at.

"That's a real eyeäble crop o' taätes. It's a good 'un."

FAGS. The lice that live in the wool of sheep.

"After I'd been shepherdin' I fun three sheep fags i' me shirt."

FORE-ELDERS. Forefathers.

" 'E belongs 'ere, but 'is fore-elders caäme from awaäy."

FROG-LOWP. (**ow** as in 'mow') Leap-frog.

"I can't frog-lowp ower you if ya doän't howd yersen firm."

GABLICK. A substantial crowbar with a point at one end and a square centre section. It was used to erect temporary netting fences to contain sheep feeding on turnips in the field. A hole was made in the ground with the point. A net-stake was inserted and then knocked firmly down by holding the gablick horizontally, the hands near both ends, and striking the top of the stake with the square centre. Then sheep netting was secured to hooks on the stakes.

GATRUM. A passage or narrow road that leads from one field to another. Sometimes it means an entrance to a field.

"We shall ha' to boon (repair with rubble) that gatrum or we shall niver git thruff it i' winter."

GAWP-SEED. (Gape-seed.) Standing with the mouth open in amazement was known as 'catching gawp-seed'.

"Doän't stand theere catchin' gawp-seed or foälks'll think ya're soft i' the 'eäd."

GAWMING. Staring.

"... and foälk stood a-gawmin' in
As thaw it wur summat bewitched isteäd of a quart o' gin."
The Northern Cobbler, Tennyson.

GAWSTER. To laugh in a loud, ribald manner.

"What do ya want to gawster like that fer? Ivrybody's gawmin' at ya."

GEE. A cry instructing a horse to turn to the right.

GISTE. To graze other people's cattle on your pasture.

"Tom wants me to giste 'is beäst till the spring fair."

GRUN. Ground. (verb)

"We hed two quarters o' barley grun at Cobb's mill for the pigs."

GRUNSOÄL. Groundsel.

"I shall ha' to weed the gardin afore the grunsoäl seeds."

GRUNSTOÄN. Grindstone.

"Come and turn the grunstoaän fer me to sharpen me tools.'

HAÄLES. The handles of a plough or wheelbarrow.

"Howd yer haäles firm if ya meän to plough straight."

HAÄMES. The lyre-shaped wooden or brass arms that fit round the collar of a horse and to which the traces are hooked.
"Them 'osses looks klink wi' their haämes all bright."

HANGICHER. Handkerchief.

"Git a clean hangicher afoäre ya goä out."

HAUVE. An instruction to a horse to turn left.

Alternatively HEAT, COME HITHER, CUBBEÄ, and MIDDA-WHOY are used in different parts of the county.

HAWM. To move about in an awkward or unseemly manner.

'Guzzlin' an' soäkin' an' smoäkin' an' hawmin' about i' the laänes.'
The Northern Cobbler, Tennyson.

HEDER AND SHEDER. A he and a she.

'Theär's heder wicken an' sheder wicken
– One's got berries, and one's got none.'
Witch Wicken, Jesse Baggaley.

HING-LOCK. A padlock. A hang-lock as opposed to one secured to a door.

HUCK. Hip.
'I slithered an' hurted my huck.'
The Northern Cobbler, Tennyson.

IZELS. Particles of soot floating about in a room, indicating that the chimney needs to be swept.
"That chimley'll ha' to be swep' 'cos theere's izels all ower the foniture."

KEDGE. Paunch. (Noun)
" 'E couldn't fasten 'is top trousers button an' 'e hed to weär a belt 'cos 'is kedge was soä big."

KELTER. Noun, rubbish. Verb, to throw away as rubbish.
n. "Chuck that kelter on the fire."
v. 'And she keltered him into the sea.'
Lincolnshire version of *The Outlandish Knight*.

KLINK. Excellent.
"I enjoyed the 'arvest supper. It was klink and soä was the singin'."

KNAP. To make a tapping sound; especially said of a door.
"Fasten that door or it will knap in the wind."

LESK. The groin.
"Iver since I lifted that weight I've hed a paäin i' me lesk."

LIMMUCK. Limp.
"If ya put a penny i' the watter it'll stop yer tulips from goin' limmuck."

LOST WI' MUCK. Filthy.
"She couldn't hev hed a wesh for weeks, fer she was lost wi' muck and stunk like a fumard." (polecat)

LOW. Small of stature.
"She was a low woman" meant that she was small, and was no reflection on her character.

MADDOCKS. Maggots. (see MAWKS)
"If ya doänt' keep the flies off that meat it'll soon be full o' maddocks.

MANTLE. To walk aimlessly up and down with short steps.
"The midwife's comin soä theere's noä need to mantle about; ya can sit yersen down."

MATTLER. A match or equal to another.
"If 'e wants to feight I'm 'is mattler."

MAWKS. Maggots. (see MADDOCKS)

"The mawks they ran ten thousands thick,
An' I couldn't knock 'em off wi' my knobbled stick."
Lincolnshire folk song, *The Farmer of Tetford.*

MIDDA-WHOY. An instruction to a horse to turn left gently.

MOG ON. Move on.

"When I'm sick o' bein' 'ere I shall mog on."

MUCKENDER. Handkerchief. (see HANGICHER)

"I got a muckender wi' a picture o' the Queen on it at the Coronation."

MUD. Might.

"I put me new dress on soä I mud ha' knawn ya was comin'."

MUN. Must.

"Git ma my aäle I tell tha, an' if I mun doy I mun doy."
Northern Farmer, Old Style, Tennyson.

NETTIN. Urine, particularly that of horses.

It was valued for 'dressing' or treating wheat before sowing, and rags soaked in nettin were tied on to a horses' swollen legs to reduce inflammation.

NOWTER. A person of no consequence. (Nowt – nothing)

"I weän't hev owt to do wi' 'im, fer 'e's a nowter."

OUTLANDISH. Beyond the bounds of normal behaviour.

" 'E drinks like a fish, smoäkes like a chimley and sweärs like a trooper. I doän't howd wi' such outlandish goings-on."

OWD STANDARDS. Old folk who have lived in a village all their lives.

"Ya wouldn't catch the owd standards playin' gaämes of a Sunday. Thaäy hed respect fer the Sabbath."

ORTS. (sometimes URTS) Left-overs on plates at the end of a meal. In certain social spheres it was customary to leave a little of each course 'for manners', but the poor considered anything not eaten as 'a saucy plate' and wasteful, so their children were taught to 'eat your orts up'.

PAG. To carry on the back.

"If you're tired I'll pag you for a bit."

The day when single farm labourers left their 'plaäces' for a new situation was known as 'Pag Rag Day' as they carried their clothes away. The date varied slightly in different areas, depending on when the local spring hiring fair was held, but it was usually about the first fortnight in May.

PAR. A chicken coop with vertical slats in the front.
The hen was confined by the slats but the chicks could get through to forage nearby.
"We must put that 'en in a par or she'll tek them chicks all ower the gardin."

PAWM. To handle needlessly.
"If ya pawm them tarts thaäy weän't be fit to eät."

POT-NODDLES. Tadpoles.
"'E 'es a jam-jar full o' pot-noddles 'e caught i' the pond."

POWER. Pour.
"Sit down an' I'll power us a cup o' tea."

RECKLIN. The smallest pig in the litter. Often applied to a weakly child.
"I hoäpe we can rear 'im, but 'e's nobbut a recklin."

REMBLE. A Danish survival that means to make tidy. A child would be told to remble his toys before going to bed, or to remble his chair at the end of a meal. i.e. to place it with the seat under the table. Tennyson, in *Northern Farmer, Old Style*, says,
'A (He) niver rembles the stoäns.'
In the Lincolnshire Wolds flints continually work their way to the surface of the soil. Good farmers had these picked off the land to assist cultivation. 'Rembling the stoäns' was a source of material for repairing roads.

SKEM. To peer intently.
"Thaäy didn't haäfe skem at my new 'at."

SLAÄPE. Slippery.
"Them roäds is slaäpe wi' ice, soä mind 'ow ya goä."

SLAP. Spill.
"That's a full bucket soä mind ya doän't slap the milk when ya carry it."

SLITHERED. Slipped.
"I slithered on the wet gress and brok me leg."

SLIVER. A blue jean or 'bluette' jacket worn by farm labourers until after the First World War.
"It was soä 'ot workin' todaäy I hed to tek me sliver off."

SMART. The smart.
A youth who 'took the Queen's shilling' when he was under the influence of drink sometimes regretted his enthusiasm when he

sobered up. He could retrieve his freedom by repaying the Recruiting Sergeant the shilling plus a pound. This was a great deal of money in the nineteenth century, so it was called 'paying the smart'.

'And keep from out the sowdger's waäy,
Thou recollects this time last year
When thou the smart was forced to paäy?"

Neddy and Sally, John Brown.

SMOOTIN. A cul-de-sac between buildings.

"If 'e runs up the smootin we can catch 'im 'cos theere's noä roäd thruff."

SMOWERED. (**ow** as in 'cow') Covered liberally all over.

"The pillow bust and we was smowered i' feathers."

SNAÄPE. To keep under control by word of command.

" 'E's a bit wild, but 'e's easy snaäped if 'e knaws ya meän it."

SNERP. To shrivel up.

"If we doän't git some räin soon them plants will snerp up."

SNICKLE. A running noose or snare.

"We'll set some snickles tonight and see if we can git a rabbit."

SNIDE. Cold, cutting weather.

"The east wind's snide this mornin'."

SPANG. To slam a door in a special way. It may be **slammed** by holding the handle, but to **spang** it is to flick it sharply so that it slams without being held.

"If ya spang the door like that ya'll fetch it off its 'inges."

SPRETCHED. Said of eggs when the hatching chick makes its first hole in the shell.

"The heggs is spretched soä the bods'll soon be out."

SQUAD. (Rhymes with 'mad') Mud.

"Wi' all the raän we've hed the laäne is squad up to the eyes."

STABBERS. The rungs of a ladder. Ladders were measured as being 'twelve stabbers' or 'eighteen stabbers' etc. long.

"Some o' the stabbers i' that lether isn't saäfe.
We shall ha' to git it mended afore somebody gits 'urt."

STAÄLE. To pass urine. Especially said of horses.

" 'E works 'is 'osses soä 'ard thaäy ain't time to staäle."

STEEL. Stile.

"If ya stand on top o' the steel ya can see the church."

STIFFENIN'. Starch.

"Put plenty o' stiffenin' i' them collars or the boss weän't be very well pleäsed."

STILT. To pull down and re-knit the feet of worn stockings or socks if the legs are still good.

"I ha' noä time to waäste. I ha three pair o' socks to stilt."

STOWP. A post.

A post hole was called a stowp-hole. Making an individual hole for each potato or broad bean being set was known as 'stowp-holin' 'em in', though it had nothing to do with posts.

A post mill in Lincolnshire was a **stowp mill.**

SWATH. (To rhyme with 'lath') The rind of bacon.

"Some foälks cuts it off, but I like to yet (eat) the swath."

TACK. Food, especially that of poor quality.

"Ya want to git some meät into ya. Bread an' jam's poor tack if ya want to do ony work."

TA'EN WORK. Taken work; piece work. Work undertaken to be done for a fixed payment.

"We allust works 'arder at ta'en work."

TATIE-TRAP. Potato trap; mouth.

A child who had been pestering his mother for a sweet was at last given one and told,

"Stick that i' your tatie-trap, and shut up "

TA-YEAR. This year.

"I reckon I'll plough that gress up ta-year."

THREAPEN. (To rhyme with 'weapon') Contradict. Sometimes curtailed to THREAP, but it usually is THREAPEN, retaining the Middle English verb ending -EN.

"Doän't threapen me when I tell ya the truth "

TIDDLEY-BUMPIN'. Tapping on a window pane with a button on a length of cotton secured to the frame by a pin. A device used by boys to annoy neighbours.

TOMMY. A loaf of bread.

"We hed better git another Tommy in caäse any company comes."

TUNNEL. Funnel.

"I can't power the paraffin into the lamps wi'out a tunnel."

TUTS. Meagre belongings.

"Ya maäy depend thaäy'll fall out ower 'er few tuts when she's deäd."

WAFF. Waft.

"If ya waff about i' front o' the fire ya'll hev the room full o' smoöke."

WEMBLE. (Normally used with 'down')

To invert a basin or saucepan on a shelf so that dust does not settle on the inside.

"When ya put that saucepan awaäy wemble it down."

WENCH-FAÄCED. Clean-shaven.

An old lady once told me, "A wench-faäced fella doesn't loök like a man."

WHOTS. Oats.

"The middle cloäse grew taäties last year, soä ta-year I shall crop it wi' whots."

WIDOW The word now refers to a female only but dialectically it was applied to either sex and qualified, e.g.,

" 'E's loänly sin' 'e's been a widow-man."
"She's a respectable widow-woman."

WIKINS. The corners of the mouth.

"We hed some hoäme maäde hot bread fer tea and theere was butter all down me wikins."

WIME ROUND. To persuade by wheedling.

"Ya wouldn't 'elp me when I wanted ya, soä doän't try to wime round me now."

WINNICK. To giggle and laugh alternately.

"Try to be serious and doaän't winnick like a little lass "

YERKS. Before wellington boots became popular farm labourers wore heavy leather footwear, and their trouser legs came over the tops of their boots so that the bottoms of their trousers easily became coated with mud. To prevent this the trouser legs were **yerked up** by securing them in pieces of twine or leather straps round the legs just below the knees. These **yerks** also prevented rats running up the inside of the trousers when corn was being threshed.

"If we work among the taäties A shall ha' to weär some yerks or A shall be loäded up wi' squad."

YET. Eat.

"Yet yer dinner up"
This is a mid Lincolnshire pronunciation. In the southern parts of the county **yet** is more usually **yeät.**

VIII

CONCLUSION

All living language is subject to change, the cumulative effect of which is considerable over long periods. The fourteenth century English of Chaucer was very different from our present day speech. He used words that have long since disappeared, like **sothly** (truly) and **wilholm** (formerly), and pronunciations that have changed considerably, especially during the Great Vowel Shift of the fifteenth century. To Chaucer 'coat' was **caut** and 'toad' was **taud,** a pronunciation we still retain in the word 'broad.'

Standard English sheds words as a tree does its leaves, but it produces new ones to take their places. Dialect also loses words, but instead of growing its own replacements it tends to borrow from current English, so over a period dialects lose their characters according to the degree to which they absorb (or are absorbed by) standard English. The dialects of Lincolnshire are today but pale shadows of their former virile characters. The time will come when dialects approach so near to standard English that they will no longer be heard in recognisable forms. Some words, phrases, and cliches will survive, but most dialect will go, leaving little but local accents and ideolects behind. While we remember the regional forms of speech with academic interest it is not desirable that we should preserve them artificially for normal use. English has a habit of taking care of itself and the dialectal variations that are likely to survive are those that continue to be used naturally in the everyday lives of the speakers. Consequently occupational dialect words will tend to survive longer than those in general use, but as working methods change under the influence of advancing technology, and as old hand tools give way to modern mechanisation the words that referred to the obsolete systems will die with them. However, modern needs produce new idioms that are characteristic of present conditions. A farm labourer driving his car may be advised to 'put yer foot down' on the accelerator, but on a tractor he would be told to 'give it some welly' (Wellington boot), but both of these instructions are English and not dialectal idioms.

Those who are interested will peruse what has been written in dialect, but most of this is of a humorous nature. There is nothing wrong with humour, though perhaps the balance should be restored by having some writers treat the dialects more seriously. Dialect is not funny just because it is dialect. It can express deep emotions as in Mabel Peacock's *Th' Lincolnsheer Poächer* (see appendix) and *The Wife A-lost* by William Barnes of Dorset, written after the death of his wife. Some rustic thoughts are better expressed in dialect than in standard English. Read Tennyson's *Northern Farmer, Old Style*, in non-dialect English and it completely loses its impact.

The dialects of today are attenuated but they are well worthy of study. While there is still time it is worthwhile to take another look at both forms of speech and to recognise that dialect has its rules as does English, though they are different. It has an ancestry at least as old and as valid as Received Pronunciation, and should not be dismissed as just debased English spoken by folk who do not know any better.

APPENDIX

Two poems are given to illustrate dialectal differences in the county.

Mabel Peacock's *Th' Lincolnsheer Poächer* was written towards the end of the nineteenth century in the speech of the Kirton Lindsey area.

Noä Callers is in the dialect of my childhood, heard in the Marshes of Lincolnshire between Louth and the coast. Normally the pronominal **A** was used for **I** and I have adhered to this rule in the poem, but occasionally it is dropped in favour of the more conventional **I.** This apparent inconsistency is deliberate as it was customary to use **I** as a more emphatic form of **A** in the First Person, Singular.

Th' Lincolnsheer Poächer

by Mabel Peacock

"Th' doctors hev' given me ower;
Thaäy tell me I mun dee
I' th' fower stoane walls o' a prison,
Wheäre ther's nowt – not a flower nor a tree;
I' th' fower stoone walls o' a prison
Wheäre a doaisy 'll niver blaw
An' nobbud gress i' th' flag stoänes
An bits o' moss 'll grow.

I'm not afeard o' deein'
But I want to hear egaän
Th' wind i' th' tops o' th' fir-trees,
An' smell th' smell o' th' raän
Wheare it cums doon streight fra heaven;
I want to hear th' call
O' th' pywipes i' th' marsh land
An' th' craws ahind th' ploo.
But thaay say them daays is ower
An' dun', fer good an' all;
I've nowt bud liggin' here waatin'
And deein' left to do.

Th' parson, he's been to seä me
Wi' a straange queer taäle to tell,
O' a narrer rough roäd to heaven
An'a stright, smoothe waäy to hell;
Bud, I think, if th' Loord wos sarten
'At He wanted us up abuv
He'd keep His roäds a bit better –
An' How can God be luv'
If He maade th' devil an' all them things
'At's creapin' an' crawlin' beloä,
Wheare, parson says, 'at unchristen'd bairns
An' mo'derers, an' such like goä?

I'm not agooin' to beleave it
O' Him 'at maade ivrything,
An' set th' sun to shine i' th' sky
An' larnt th' bo'ds to sing;
Bud I'd raythen be doon wheare th' fire
An' brimstun foriver bo'ns'
An' just goä roond wi' a bucket
An' give fook drinks by to'ns –
Then sit i' yon stright maade heaven,
Wheare saints an' aängels sing,

An' niver hear a pheasant craw,
Nor th' skirr o' a partridge wing;
Wheare ther' isn't a bank nor a plantin'-side
Wheare rabbits cum oot on' plaay,
An' stamp wi' ther' feet o' a moonleet neet,
Wheare it's warm o' th' coudest daay;
An' th' otchins ligs hid i' winter –
Ther's nowt like this, i doot –
Why, them 'at gets sent up to heaven
Mun be stolled when a week's runn'd oot.

It's a weary while I've been liggin'
Wi' my faace to a prison wall,
But I knaw ootside th' black heäds cry
An' it' spring, on' th' cuckoos call:–
I' not afeard o' deein'
But I straangely want to see
Th' sun com up ower Ranthrup
Agaan afore I dee."

Noä Callers

by G. Edward Campion

Cum in, lass, A'm real pleased to see ya,
yah're welcome as flowers i' Maäy.
Cum an' sit yersen down o' the soäfy –
not that end – a bit tother waäy;
The cushions is clean an' A doän't want 'm ruckled,
thaäy're fresh weshed ya see.
A doän't oftens git many callers,
soä A'm glad that yah've comed to see me.

A likes to keep things niste and tidy,
not like some foälks what lives i' the Laäne,
Theere's owd Mrs. Brown an' 'er dowter,
thaäy're mucky as sin an' it's plaäin
That thaäy niver not wesh theirsens proper
fer thaäy stinks like a fumard. Soä be
A weän't 'ev 'em sit o' *my* cushions,
soä thaäy niver not comes to see me.

Then theere's 'er at the corner, the thin 'un,
an' thaäy saäy she can sup moöre than moäst,
An' A 'ears as 'ow when she was younger
that she wasn't perticler. Thaäy boäst

---

otchins - hedgehogs: fumard - polecat

I' the pub, when thaäy're well on wi' drinkin',
    of 'ow wi' the men she was free.
I telled 'er I doän't howd wi sinnin',
    soä she niver cums to see me.

Then Aäda, that's 'er wi' green curtains;
    haäfe ower the winder thaäy're drawn
Soä as noän can see in, but she stan's theere
    skemmin' round 'em as soon as it's dawn.
She knaws ower much, an' like moäst foälks
    round 'ere she's as daft as can be,
Goän soft i' the 'eäd. I doän't trust 'er.
    A weän't 'ev 'er in to see me!

An' 'im as lives theere wi' is muther,
    wheere the door's paäinted yaller an' black;
Dressed up to the nines 'e goäs out ivery night,
    an' A niver knaws when 'e cums back.
A can't reckon what 'e gits up to,
    but it's nowt very good. Theere 'e be
Done up like a Duke, I calls 'im Lord Muck,
    an' 'e niver cums to see me.

Th'owd parson's a bit of a nowter.
    Last Christmas thaäy browt boxes round
To all us owd foälks i' the village,
    but mine was woth under a pound.
Now 'er as 'es six bairns, the widder,
    got fower times moöre, an' all free!
I telled the owd parson that it wasn't reight.
    Now 'e niver cums to see me.

A'd best put the kettle on – now then,
    wheere was A? Lord, just loök yah theere!
Theere's three o' the owd laädy's grandbairns
    goän gallopin' in. Dear-a dear!
She's a deal ower owd to loök after
    one bairn, let aloän two or three,
While their muther's out workin'. I telled 'er,
    soä she niver cums to see me.

How's yer muther ? A've knawn 'er a long while,
    sin' she got into trouble at Bourne
Fer bein' light-fingered i' sarvice.
    She niver knawed what was 'er awn.
An' 'er wi' the maäster's son, 'Enry –
    Yah're not leävin' that cup o' tea!
Yah must git agaäte or yah're goin to be laäte?
    Well, cum ageän soon and see me!

SUGGESTIONS FOR FURTHER READING

1. English Dialects, G. L. Brook. Andre Deutsch, 1963.

2. Fourteenth Century Verse and Prose, (With glossary), Kenneth Sisam. Oxford University Press 1970 Edn.

3. Glossary of Words Used in the Wapentakes of Manley and Corringham, Lincolnshire, Edward Peacock, F.S.A. Second Edn. 1889. Published for the English Dialect Society by Trubner & Co., Ludgate Hill.

4. Growth and Structure of the English Language, Otto Jespersen, Ph.D., Lit. D., LL.D. Basil Blackwell Oxford. 1962.

5. A History of the English Language, Albert C. Baugh, Professor of English, University of Pennsylvania. Routledge & Kegan Paul, Ltd., London. Second Edn. 1959.

6. A Lincolnshire Glossary, Jabez Good. Reprinted by C. H. Major & Co. Ltd., Skegness.

7. Lincolnshire and the Danes, G. S. Streatfleld, M.A. Kedgan Paul, Trench & Co. 1884.

8. Middle-English Dictionary, F. H. Stratmann. Oxford University Press. 1891. Reprinted 1971.

9. A Tennsyon Dialect Glossary, G. Edward Campion. Published by Lincolnshire and Humberside Arts. 1969.

10. Changing English, Simeon Potter. The Language Library Andre Deutsch.

Publisher's Note

When this small book on the Lincolnshire dialects was first published in 1976 a 'Publisher's Note' was added detailing sources of other books of particular 'Lincolnshire interest' and indicating from where they could be obtained. These details have changed considerably in the 18 years that have elapsed since then and this note is merely to update that information – it is not in any way a comprehensive guide.

The Society for Lincolnshire History and Archaeology has moved to: Jews Court, Steep Hill, LINCOLN. LN2 1LS (Tel. 0522 521337) where they have an extensive bookshop of Local historical publications. (Open: Tuesday – Saturday 10.00 am – 4.00 pm).

There are also several small publishers of material relevant to Lincolnshire in general: The Lincolnshire C. C. (through the Lincolnshire Libraries), Lincolnshire Heritage, especially for its *Lincolnshire from the Air*,

The Lincolnshire and Humberside Arts was absorbed into Eastern Arts (based in Cambridge) and their publications dispersed to authors and various societies and groups. We have a few remaining copies of many of their publications and dialect records (45 and 33 rpm). At present we have some copies of most of the Lincolnshire Folk Songs. We are glad to do what we can to answer any queries.

We now publish and distribute a number of books associated with the county of Lincolnshire ranging from those which are specifically orientated to a county interest – such as our dialect titles – to those which, whilst having a particular county association, have a significance extending far beyond Lincolnshire — and indeed sometimes far beyond Britain — titles such as *William Brewster: The Father of New England* which is a detailed examination of the causes, origins, and early years of the Separatist Church, both in England and The Netherlands, and the first two decades of the Pilgrim Fathers in America.

Our **Life in Lincolnshire** titles, whilst being directly Lincolnshire in that they are (auto)biographical accounts of some aspect of life in the county, are also of much wider interest. Although they do stem from a Lincolnshire setting their relevance is not at all confined to within county boundaries but rather to the times in which they are set in an English county. They range from the steelworks of Scunthorpe and the trawling industry of Grimsby in the north (the historic Lincolnshire and likely soon again to return) to the farming of the south and much in between. These are all factual and not fiction. Our **Vernacular History** titles (just commencing publication) are similar but usually shorter, and often more colloquial. They are often (but not invariably) the work of those who are less accustomed to expressing themselves by means of the written word.

Our full catalogue is available on request
(see also inside the back cover)

Tel. 0205 353231

RICHARD KAY PUBLICATIONS
80 Sleaford Road • Boston • Lincs. • PE21 8EU

OTHER LINCOLNSHIRE DIALECT BOOKS

Lincoln Fair – a small anthology of the poetry of Bernard Gilbert edited by Patrick O'Shaughnessy and illustrated by Jenny Reynish. Pb'k at present O/P – Cased £10.00

Fungus the Lincolnshire Cat by Fred Dobson: illustrated by Jenny Reynish

Stories about an imaginary cat with the gift of occasional speech—in the Lincolnshire dialect! Pb'k £2.75/Hb'k £3.95

Lincolnshire Folk by Fred Dobson with cartoons by 'Dav' (John Blundy) – a small saddlestitched booklet of verse and sketches in dialect. £1.95

Lincolnshirics
Fred Dobson with cartoons by 'Dav' £1.50

Later this year we hope to issue a collection of words and phrases recently in current use in the area of Kirton (Holland) and collected over the years by Ken Pearson.

Also later this year, or early in 1995, we hope to publish the most comprehensive *Dictionary of the Lincolnshire Dialects* so far accumulated—some 6,500 words with 10,000 meanings: the result of several years work by Mrs Joan Sims.

AND MANY OTHER LINCOLNSHIRE BOOKS

In addition to the dialect titles we have many titles of wider Lincolnshire interest. These include our **Life in Lincolnshire** titles which range from deep sea fishing to fen farming and many in between. We have three titles on the Civil War in Lincolnshire and others of that period.

We published *The Royal Navy in Lincolnshire* in 1992 and soon hope to issue *Crossroad in the Air:* a comprehensive survey of everything that has happened in the air in the fens (not solely Lincolnshire) – from the first hot-air balloons to supersonic flight. [See also p. 63]

OUR FULL CATALOGUE IS AVAILABLE ON REQUEST